DATE DUE

Artists in Their Time

Andy Warhol

Linda Bolton

Franklin Watts
A Division of Scholastic Inc.
New York Toronto London Auckland Sydney
Mexico City New Delhi Hong Kong
Danbury, Connecticut

First published in 2002 by
Franklin Watts
96 Leonard Street
London EC2A 4XD

First American edition published
in 2002 by Franklin Watts
A Division of Scholastic Inc.
90 Sherman Turnpike
Danbury, CT 06816

Series Editor: Adrian Cole
Series Designer: Mo Choy
Art Director: Jonathan Hair
Picture Researcher: Julie McMahon

A CIP catalog record for this title
is available from the Library of Congress.

ISBN 0-531-12225-5 (Lib. Bdg.)
ISBN 0-531-16618-X (Pbk.)

Printed in Hong Kong, China

Acknowledgements

AKG London: 15 © The Andy Warhol Foundation for the Visual Arts, Inc./ARS, NY and DACS, London 2002 & © 2002 Ronald Feldman Fine Arts, NY; 19 © The Andy Warhol Foundation for the Visual Arts, Inc./ARS, NY and DACS, London 2002; 29 © The Andy Warhol Foundation for the Visual Arts, Inc./ARS, NY and DACS, London 2002; 42. Archives of The Andy Warhol Museum, Pittsburgh: 6; 7t; 9t; 22b; 32, 39 © The Andy Warhol Foundation for the Visual Arts, Inc./ARS, NY and DACS, London 2002; 41b Paul Rocheleau. Artothek: 14 © The Estate of Roy Lichtenstein/DACS 2002. BFI Collections: 35 © The Andy Warhol Foundation for the Visual Arts, Inc./ARS, NY and DACS, London 2002. Courtesy of Collection Stephanie Seymour Brant, The Brant Foundation, Greenwich, CT: 11 © The Andy Warhol Foundation for the Visual Arts, Inc./ARS, NY and DACS, London 2002; 31 © The Andy Warhol Foundation for the Visual Arts, Inc./ARS, NY and DACS, London 2002. Bridgeman /Private Collection 13t © Robert Rauschenberg/DACS, London/VAGA, New York 2002. Bridgeman/Saatchi Collection, London 17 & cover centre © The Andy Warhol Foundation for the Visual Arts, Inc./ARS, NY and DACS, London 2002. Trademarks Licensed by Campbell Soup Company. All Rights Reserved. Bridgeman/Henry N Abrams Family Collection 18c © The Andy Warhol Foundation for the Visual Arts, Inc./ARS, NY and DACS, London 2002; Bridgeman/Hungarian National Gallery, Budapest 21 © The Andy Warhol Foundation for the Visual Arts, Inc./ARS, NY and DACS, London 2002. Bridgeman/Private Collection 28c © Succession Marcel Duchamp/ADAGP, Paris and DACS London 2002. Carnegie Mellon University Archives: 9b. Christie's Images Ltd: 25 © The Andy Warhol Foundation for the Visual Arts, Inc./ ARS, NY and DACS, London 2002; 37 © The Andy Warhol Foundation for the Visual Arts, Inc./ARS, NY and DACS, London 2002. The Coca Cola Company: 12b/Advertising Archives. Condé Nast NY: 10c Vogue Cover/Advertising Archives. Corbis: 16t Bettman; 23 Burstein Collection © The Andy Warhol Foundation for the Visual Arts, Inc./ARS, NY and DACS, London 2002; 34c Bettman; 36t Lynn Goldsmith; 40 Liba Taylor. Culver Pictures: 8. Edifice: 41t Lewis-Darley. General Motors Corporation 2002: 24b used with permission of GM Media Archives/Advertising Archives. Ronald Grant Archive: 27. Hulton/Archive: Cover bl & 10t; 12t; 13b; 22t; 24t; 28b; 30b; 33t Santi Visalli Inc; 33b; 34t. Robert Hunt Library: 7b. Kobal Collection: 18t & cover bc 20th Century Fox; 38t. Popperfoto: 30t. Pittsburgh Post-Gazette: 38b Mark Murphy. Redferns: 20t & b. Rex Features: 36b & cover br. Stephen Shore: 16b; 26t & b.

Whilst every attempt has been made to clear copyright
should there be any inadvertent omission please apply
in the first instance to the publisher regarding rectification.

Contents

Who Was Andy Warhol?

Andy Warhol was one of the most influential American artists of the 20th century. His art and his lifestyle reflected the rapidly changing culture of his time.

As a young boy Warhol was obsessed with fame and glamour. He read fan magazines about Hollywood film stars, and collected autograph pictures and newspaper cuttings about them. He went to his local movie theater to watch all the latest films, which increased his interest in the Hollywood lifestyle of the rich and famous.

"I was very much part of my times, of my culture, as much a part of it as rockets and television."

Andy Warhol

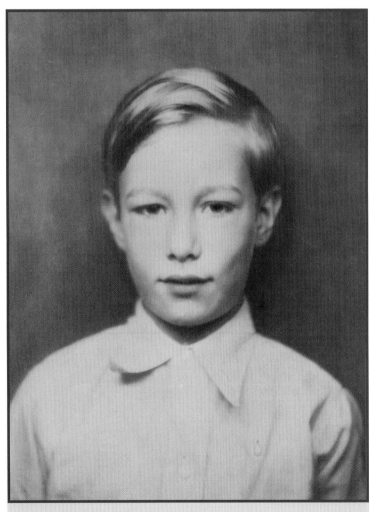

▲ This hand-colored photograph shows Andrew Warhola, (as Andy Warhol was known then), at age eight.

POP ART, POP ARTIST

As he grew older, Warhol transformed this obsession into art. He is famous for the prints he made showing celebrities, including the film star Marilyn Monroe and the rock and roll singer Elvis Presley. He also focused on name brand products such as Campbell's soup and Brillo soap pads. These were all part of the popular culture of the time, and the subject of what became known as the "Pop" artists. Warhol was probably the greatest Pop artist of them all.

The silk-screen technique he used produced very brightly colored prints. It was a commercial process that allowed him to print multiple copies of each artwork on a printing press.

Warhol also made films. They were not mainstream films like the ones at the local movie theater, with lots of characters and a storyline. His films sometimes lasted for hours and might only feature a single person.

FAME

Warhol also wrote many books and produced a magazine called *Interview*. As the name suggests, this magazine published interviews with celebrities from the world of rock and pop music, film and art, and literature and politics.

By the mid-1960s Warhol was the most famous artist in the U.S. Around the world, he was often more famous than the celebrities he painted.

► Warhol (on the left), with his mother Julia, his aunt Mrs. Preksta, and her stepson George Guke, 1937.

▲ A photograph of a village in the same area as Mikova, c.1905. At the time, such villages were harsh places to grow up in and many people wanted to emigrate.

FAMILY BACKGROUND

Warhol's parents both emigrated to the U.S. from the village of Mikova, in what is today Slovakia (formerly part of Czechoslovakia).

His father, Ondrej Warhola, first arrived in 1909, but then returned to Mikova to find a wife. He married Julia Zavachy and went back to the U.S. in 1913. Julia had to stay behind to look after her younger sisters. The start of World War I, in 1914, delayed her departure further. It wasn't until 1921, eight years later, that she was able to join her husband in Pittsburgh, Pennsylvania. In those days Pittsburgh was an important center for the steel and coal industry. Other family members also lived there, including one of Ondrej's brothers, two of Julia's sisters, and two of her brothers.

Ondrej was a hard-working miner and construction worker. He and Julia had three sons, Paul, John, and the youngest, Andrew.

Early Life

Andy Warhol was born Andrew Warhola in Forest City, Pennsylvania, on August 6, 1928. Later he claimed that his birth certificate was wrong and that he was born in 1930, or even 1931. However, most people think that this was an attempt to add mystery and interest to his early life.

Warhol's father worked away from home a lot, and his mother cared for the three boys on her own through the difficult years of the Great Depression and World War II.

▲ The steel and coal industries dominated the landscape of Forest City. The area was poor and largely made up of immigrant families from Eastern Europe.

"She'd give me a Hershey Bar every time I finished a page in my coloring book."

Andy Warhol, about his mother

In 1942, when Warhol was 14, his father died after a long illness. The family was poor but all the boys worked hard and saved what money they could from their part-time and summer jobs.

STUDENT DAYS

Warhol had always been interested in art. In 1945, he graduated from high school and went to study pictorial design at Pittsburgh's famous Carnegie Institute of Technology (known as CIT). One of his fellow students there was Philip Pearlstein (b.1924). Pearlstein remembers that Warhol often came over to his house to study, saying that it was too crowded and difficult to study at home.

TIMELINE ▶

August 6, 1928	1942	1945	1945-49
Andrew Warhola is born in Forest City, Pennsylvania.	Ondrej Warhola dies after a three-year illness. Andy Warhol goes on to finish high school.	World War II ends.	Warhol studies pictorial design at the Carnegie Institute of Technology in Pittsburgh. Meets Philip Pearlstein, a fellow student. Warhol works during the holidays in a department store, and makes first visit to New York City.

During the summer, Warhol had to work to earn his keep. He wrote, "I had a job one summer in a department store looking through *Vogue* and *Harper's Bazaar* and European fashion magazines for a wonderful man named Mr. Vollmer. I got something like 50 cents an hour and my job was to look for "ideas." I don't remember ever finding one or getting one. Mr. Vollmer was an idol to me because he came from New York and that seemed so exciting."

LEAVING FOR NEW YORK

In June of 1949, Warhol graduated with a degree in Fine Arts. He planned on becoming an art teacher. During the summer, however, Pearlstein persuaded him to go to New York. The two men set off, uncertain about how they would manage in the big city.

From New York, Warhol sent a postcard home to his mother everyday and went to church at least twice a week. (In 1952, Julia Warhola joined her son in New York. She remained there until her death 20 years later at the age of 80.)

Soon Warhol had decided not to pursue a teaching career but wanted to try and interest magazines in his artwork instead. The work he

▲ Philip Pearlstein (on the left) and Andy Warhol photographed with a woman friend at Rockefeller Center, New York, c.1949.

showed them was a development of what he had been doing as a picture editor for the CIT student magazine, *Cano*. Over the next 11 years the prints Warhol produced, with their smudged lines, were to become his trademark style.

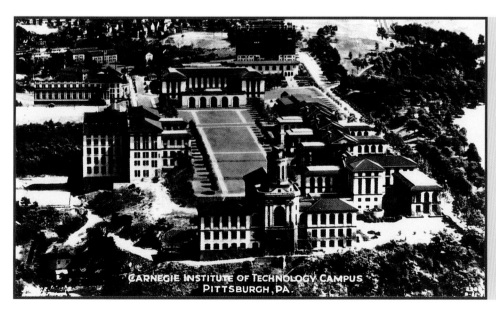

◀ Carnegie Institute of Technology campus. Warhol failed perspective drawing at CIT, but attended a summer course to make the grade. He graduated on June 16, 1949.

The Big Apple

▲ The Statue of Liberty, a symbol of New York.

For Andy Warhol, New York was magical. During his first summer there, in 1949, he tried to interest magazine publishers in his work. Tina Fredericks, at *Glamour* magazine, liked Warhol's drawings but only needed drawings of shoes. Warhol returned the following day with 50 drawings of shoes. Tina used his drawings to illustrate an article called "Success Is a Job in New York" in the September issue of the magazine.

From then on Warhol made footwear one of the subjects of his art. His series "Golden Shoes" paid tribute to many of his favorite stars, featuring them all in the form of shoes.

NEW YORK

By 1950, New York had become the largest city in the world with a population of over 13 million. Wall Street was at the center of international trade. New York's port – overlooked by the Statue of Liberty – supplied goods all over the world. New York was also the center of magazine and book publishing, theater (on Broadway), and showbusiness. The island of Manhattan, with its exclusive shops and restaurants, was the backbone of American high society. It's no wonder that proud New Yorkers called their city "the Big Apple."

◄ A cover for the fashion magazine *Vogue*, issue dated June 1958. The cover is typical of 1950s' design in the way it uses simple illustrations rather than the glossy color photographs we use today.

Commercial art was in great demand in the 1950s and helped launch Warhol's career.

It did not take long for Warhol to become a successful commercial artist. He created advertisements for magazines such as *Glamour* and *Vogue*, window displays for department stores, illustrations for record companies such as RCA, and various commercial advertising campaigns. In 1956, he won the Annual Art Directors' Club Award for his advertisement for I. Miller Shoes and was invited to exhibit his work.

Warhol was very encouraged by this. Toward the end of the 1950s he had begun to realize that he wanted to become a serious artist, not just a commercial artist.

TIMELINE ▶

1949	1952	1954	1956
Warhol is employed as a commercial artist for *Vogue* and *Harper's Bazaar*, produces his first advertising drawings for I. Miller and creates window displays for the department store Bonwit Teller. He shortens his name to Andy Warhol.	Warhol exhibits at the Hugo Gallery, New York. His mother comes to New York.	Warhol's first group exhibition at the Loft Gallery, New York.	Warhol wins the 36th Annual Art Directors' Club Award for an I. Miller shoe advertisement.

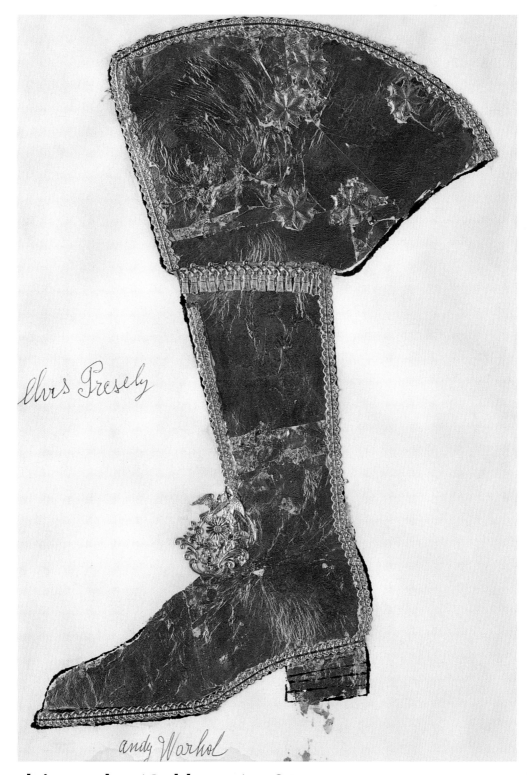

Elvis Presley (Gold Boot), 1956
ink, gold leaf, collage on paper, 20 x 14 in (50.8 x 35.6 cm), The Brant Foundation, Greenwich, Connecticut

In his "Golden Shoes" series, Warhol depicted various stars in the form of shoes.
Other stars featured in the series include Judy Garland, Julie Andrews, and James Dean.

Pop Art

Popular art, also know as Pop art, emerged in the mid-1950s. It drew its inspiration from the images of popular culture and consumer society – advertisements, magazines, billboards, cartoon strips, pop music, television, and film stars.

Some Pop artists used their art to criticize the consumer society. Others, like Warhol, neither criticized nor praised, but simply reflected the things around them at the time. Warhol, for example, painted everyday products – such as Campbell's soup cans, Coca-Cola bottles, and Brillo Pad boxes – that had a clear brand design.

▲ An American family shopping, 1950s. The 1950s marked the start of what became known as the consumer society.

IMAGES FROM MASS CULTURE

The term "Pop art" was first used in 1957, in a meeting about fashion, mass media, science fiction, industrial design, and other related subjects at the Institute of Contemporary Arts (ICA) in London.

By the end of the 1950s a group of artists including Andy Warhol, Roy Lichtenstein (b.1923), Claes Oldenburg (b.1929), and Tom Wesselmann (b.1931) were creating images based on television commercials, cartoon strips, and advertising billboards. To produce their art, they often used commercial mass-production techniques such as silk-screen printing.

> *"Buying is much more American than thinking, and I'm as American as they come."*
> *Andy Warhol*

▲ A 1950s advertisement for Coca-Cola, then sold in distinctive shaped bottles. The brand logo at the top of the advertisement is instantly recognizable. Brands such as this were very attractive to the Pop artists.

ART FOR EVERYBODY

Although never a formal group, Pop artists wanted to produce art for everybody. They used subjects that were familiar in everyday life, such as name brand products and newspaper photographs.

This idea was immediately successful. Early exhibitions of Pop art received an enthusiastic response from the public. People felt like they were able to understand the art, even though its meaning was often deliberately unclear.

POP ART AND ABSTRACT EXPRESSIONISM

In many ways, Pop art was a reaction to the Abstract Expressionism which had dominated the U.S. art scene during the late 1940s and early '50s.

Abstract Expressionism – art which communicates the artist's emotional state through expressive but abstract marks – was practiced by artists such as Jackson Pollock (1912-56) and Robert Rauschenberg (b.1925). During the '50s Rauschenberg changed his ideas and began painting Coca-Cola bottles, electric fans, and radios in much the same way as the Pop artists were doing.

▲ *#66 Double Feature*, Robert Rauschenberg, 1959.
This picture was made using paint, textiles, and printed matter.

▲ Eating hot dogs, 1950s. Hot dogs were one of the first "fast foods" widely available from roadside "fast food" stands and eaten on the move. They became a symbol of the consumer society, which did not have time to wait for a sit-down meal.

In their attempt to create art for everyone, the young Pop artists were reacting to the difficult and often obscure style of Abstract Expressionism. They deliberately tried not to use their art to express their own thoughts and feelings, and replaced the serious ideas of Abstract Expressionism with images from the consumer society. For example, instead of thinking about how to represent the human soul in paint, the Pop artists showed hot dogs; instead of depicting anger and fear, they had a shopping basket; instead of passion, for them there was popcorn.

Leonard Kesseler, one of Warhol's fellow students at the Carnegie Institute of Technology, remembered having the following conversation with Warhol in New York:
Kesseler: "Andy! What are you doing?"
Warhol: "I'm starting Pop art."
Kesseler: "Why?"
Warhol: "Because I hate Abstract Expressionism. I hate it!"

Cartoon Strips

In 1960-61 Warhol began to make paintings based on cartoon strips. He was unaware that another American artist, Roy Lichtenstein (b.1923), was also creating paintings from blown-up comic book illustrations. Simultaneously but separately, the two artists had the same idea of depicting commercial images on a very large scale.

Warhol felt frustrated. In 1961 he told his friend, the interior designer Muriel Latow, "I've got to do something that will have a lot of impact, that will be different from Lichtenstein. I don't know what to do!" He paid Latow $50 to give him a new idea.

She asked, "What do you like most in the whole world?" and then told him, "Money. You should paint pictures of money ... Or paint something that everybody sees everyday, that everybody recognizes ... like a can of soup."

Warhol smiled. He had his inspiration. The very next morning he sent his mother out to buy one of the 32 varieties of Campbell's soup.

"Pop art was just man-made ... Andy was there at the right time when they wanted to expose art a little."

Paul Warhola, Warhol's brother

▲ *Hopeless*, **Roy Lichtenstein, 1963.** Seen from a distance; the big dots of color Lichtenstein used merge into one another.

ROY LICHTENSTEIN (B.1923)

Roy Lichtenstein first exhibited his blown-up cartoons in 1962. They were a huge success, proving equally popular with the public and the critics.

Although both artists used images from popular culture, Lichtenstein's style was quite different from Warhol's. Lichtenstein painted with large dots of bright color to give the impression of a solid block of color – in much the same way as commercial printing does.

TIMELINE ▶

1957	September 1960	1960	1961	1962
Warhol has plastic surgery to change the shape of his nose.	Warhol moves to 1342 Lexington Avenue.	Warhol begins to paint pictures using blown-up cartoon strips.	Warhol creates his first pictures of Campbell's soup cans.	Lichtenstein exhibits his cartoon artwork at Leo Castelli's gallery in New York.

Superman, 1960

casein and wax crayon on cotton, 67 x 52 in (170.2 x 132.1 cm), Gunter Sachs Collection

The cartoon-strip hero Superman was always a popular choice for artists trying to introduce modern images into their art. Many of Warhol's contemporaries also painted their versions of Superman, including Philip Pearlstein, Jasper Johns, Robert Rauschenberg, and Roy Lichtenstein.

Soup Star

SILK-SCREEN PRINTING

Around 1962, Warhol started using the photographic silk-screen process for printing his work.

This was adapted from the traditional silk-screen technique in which a stencil is cut out, placed against a sheet of framed mesh, and then colored ink is forced through the mesh onto the paper underneath.

Photographic silk-screen uses a photochemical process to transfer a photographic image onto a screen. During printing, colors can be changed and many versions of the same image can be made.

◀ Warhol (right) with a number of friends. The opening night of a new exhibition was not just a chance to look at the works of art on display. It also provided an opportunity to socialize.

In 1962, at the Ferus Gallery in Los Angeles, Warhol showed 32 paintings of Campbell's soup cans. Their style came to identify his art.

The initial public reaction was disappointing. An art dealer mocked Warhol by displaying a stack of real soup cans nearby, with a sign reading, "Get the real thing for 29 cents."

The response to the soup cans was poor in Los Angeles, but sensational in New York. They were the stars of the show, and completely different from what any other artists were creating. Warhol said that the soup cans reminded him of his childhood when he ate Campbell's tomato soup daily. They remain bold images of American consumer society.

▲ Warhol (left) had many assistants to help create his prints.

PRINTING THE IMAGES

In the summer of 1962, Warhol began experimenting with a commercial printing technique by using silk-screens (see left panel). "The reason I'm painting this way is because I want to be a machine. I tried doing them by hand, but I find it easier to use a screen. This way, I don't have to work on my objects at all. One of my assistants or anyone else, for that matter, can reproduce the design as well as I could."

TIMELINE ▶

Summer 1962	August 1962	September-October 1962	October 1962
Warhol creates his first pictures using silk-screen printing.	Warhol exhibits 32 pictures of Campbell's soup cans at the Ferus Gallery in Los Angeles. Because of lack of interest, he buys them all himself.	The Cuban missile crisis brings the world close to nuclear war after the U.S. discovers Russian nuclear missiles in Cuba.	Warhol displays his work at the Pop Art exhibition "The New Realists" at the Sidney Janis Gallery, New York.

Soup Can, 1962

casein and pencil on linen, 8 $^2/_3$ x 6 $^2/_3$ in (22 x 17 cm), Saatchi Collection, London, England

Although he produced several versions, Warhol's soup cans were never identical. As well as different types of soup, the colors of the cans change, there are subtle changes to the lettering, sometimes the cans are open and sometimes closed, and some even have prices on them as if they had just been bought off the supermarket shelf.

Hollywood Blonde

In August of 1962, the film star Marilyn Monroe died of a drug overdose. By the end of that year Warhol had made 23 prints of her, all based on a publicity shot for her 1953 film *Niagara*. Warhol experimented with different color schemes, painting Monroe against backgrounds of gold, orange, or purple, and giving her blue, green, or purple eyeshadow. Silk-screen printing made it easy for him to try these changes.

Between August and December of 1962, Warhol produced around 2,000 pictures, including some of his most famous images. Over the next ten years he continued to work on them and reproduced them again and again.

▲ Marilyn Monroe in a scene from the movie *Gentlemen Prefer Blondes*.

A HOLLYWOOD ICON

Marilyn Monroe's real name was Norma Jean Baker. Born in Los Angeles in 1926, she spent most of her childhood in foster care. In 1946 she became a model, and in 1953 starred as a "dumb blonde" in the first of many films, which include *How to Marry a Millionaire* and *Gentlemen Prefer Blondes*. After her early death in 1962, she came to symbolize Hollywood's abuse of youth and beauty.

Warhol was fascinated by both death and celebrities, so Monroe was a natural subject for him.

◀ *Green Coca-Cola Bottles*, Andy Warhol, 1962. This picture was exhibited at the Stable Gallery in 1962. It graphically illustrates how one image, in this case the classic Coca-Cola bottle, can be used to produce a visually exciting work of art.

In November of 1962, Warhol had his first solo exhibition at the Stable Gallery in Manhattan, New York. Both the public and art critics loved his work. Andy Warhol became famous overnight.

In the show, Warhol included his pictures of Coca-Cola bottles, Campbell's soup cans, and dollar bills. He also included his portraits of Marilyn Monroe.

TIMELINE ▶

August 5, 1962	Autumn 1962	November 6-24, 1962
Marilyn Monroe is found dead at her home in Hollywood.	Warhol begins the first prints in his "Marilyn" series.	Warhol has his first solo exhibition at Eleanor Ward's Stable Gallery in New York.

Lavender Marilyn, 1962
silk-screen ink and acrylic on linen, 20 x 16 in (50.8 x 40.6 cm), Private Collection, Stuttgart, Germany

Warhol's portraits of Marilyn Monroe focused particularly on those features that had made her beautiful, her large red lips, her eyes (especially the color of her eyeshadow), and her thick blonde hair.

"The King"

In the 1950s popular music began to cater to a new consumer, the "teenager" – a word first used in the '50s – and pop music was born.

Pop music had mass appeal and included many styles. The most famous, rock and roll, was a mixture of traditional American rhythm and blues, and country and western.

During the '60s, under the influence of hippie culture, pop music changed and many new bands were formed. Warhol became associated with a band called Velvet Underground in 1964. He later designed a sleeve for their album *Velvet Underground and Nico*.

Elvis Presley (1935-77) quickly earned the nickname "Elvis the Pelvis" because of his hip-swinging stage performances. These performances excited American teenage fans and shocked their disapproving parents.

Elvis also made a number of movies, including *Loving You* (1957), *King Creole* (1958), and *GI Blues* (1960), that were huge box office successes.

In the '50s and early '60s Elvis was more than a great rock and roll star. He was also a symbol of the new postwar America and hero to a whole generation who called him "the King."

Elvis Presley was born in Tupelo, Mississippi, in 1935. After graduating from high school, where he sang in his church choir, he went to work as a truck driver. In 1953 he began recording for Sun Records in Memphis, Tennessee. He went on to become one of the greatest rock and roll singers of all time and the first teenage idol.

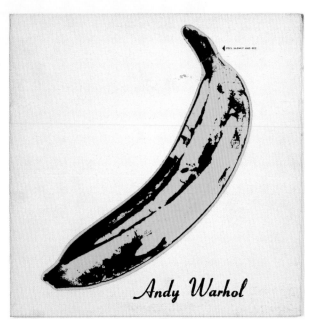

▲ Andy Warhol designed this cover for the album *Velvet Underground and Nico* in 1967.

POP ICON

With his blue jeans, leather jacket, T-shirt, chewing gum, and slicked-back hair, Elvis represented a new kind of culture. Warhol knew this and featured Elvis repeatedly, using his popularity but at the same time contributing to it. As he had done for his "Marilyn" prints, Warhol experimented with various color and image combinations, visually achieving very different pictures based on the same silk-screen image.

Elvis (right) is just one of many versions produced by Warhol. In this example he sprayed the canvas with silver car paint before printing the silk-screen image. Other pictures show the image of Elvis reproduced two or more times in one picture.

Elvis, 1963
silk-screen ink and silver paint on linen, 82 x 35 in (208.3 x 91.4 cm),
Hungarian National Gallery, Budapest, Hungary

This image of Elvis emphsizes his status as an icon of American youth culture by almost appearing too large for the page.

Death and Disaster

▲ **Watching TV, 1960s.** Television brought images of death and disaster right into people's living rooms.

In contrast to his celebrity pictures, Warhol was also fascinated by another side of American life, far from the fame and glamour of showbusiness. Warhol said that it was his friend Henry Geldzahler who provided the inspiration for his "Death and Disaster" series: "We were having lunch one day in the summer ... and he laid a newspaper out on the table. The headline was '129 DIE IN JET!' And that's what started me on the death series – the Car Crashes, the Disasters, the Electric Chairs ..."

CAPTURING THE DISASTER

Warhol produced a whole series of pictures based on press photographs of real-life disasters, some of which had not even been used in the newspapers because they were too gruesome. Using the silk-screen printing process, he produced multiple versions of the same image without making any comment on how he felt or how he expected others to feel. In his view, the pictures were powerful enough for people to make up their own minds.

REPEATING IMAGES

Many of the pictures in the "Death and Disaster" series feature the same image used over and over again in a grid pattern. Warhol said he did this because he believed in quantity rather than quality, a phrase he borrowed from industry.

Repeating something many times changed the way people reacted to it. Repetition and multiple images became an important feature of Warhol's art and reflected a society bombarded by images.

"When you see a gruesome picture over and over again, it doesn't really have an effect."

Andy Warhol

◀ The original front cover of the headline "129 DIE IN JET!" that started Warhol's interest in images of death and destruction. To make his disaster pictures, Warhol generally used a mixture of newspaper photos and headlines which he projected onto a screen.

TIMELINE ▶

June 1962	September 1962	Autumn 1962	1962-63
An article in a newspaper inspires Warhol to produce his "Death and Disaster" series.	Warhol moves to the Firehouse on East 87th Street, New York.	Warhol begins work on the first of his "Disaster" pictures.	Warhol produces the first of his "Car Crash" scenes.

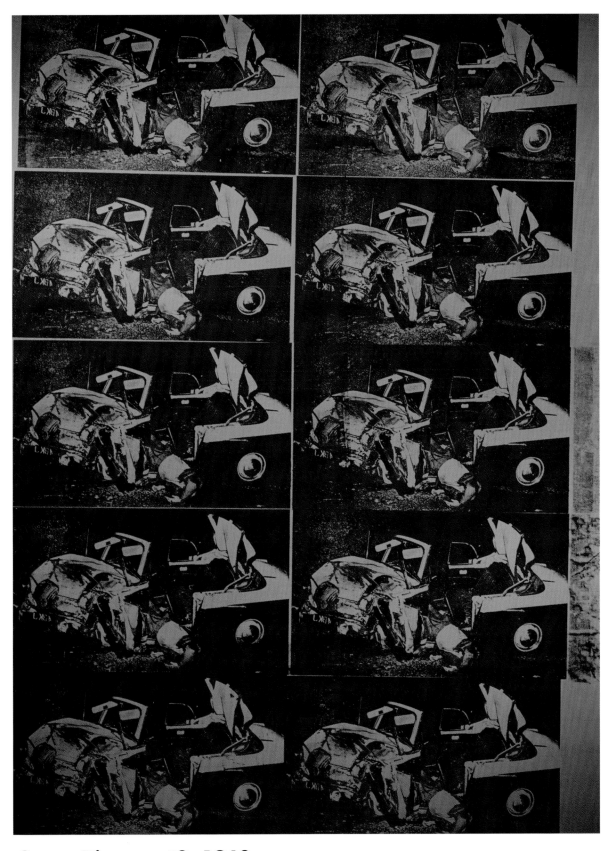

Green Disaster #2, 1963
acrylic and silk-screen ink on canvas, 30 x 23 in (76.2 x 58.6 cm), Burstein Collection

Warhol used powerful, hard-hitting pictures that summed up the way society was becoming so used to images of horror that they were no longer shocked by them.

American Contrasts

▲ Martin L. King Jr. in Washington, D.C., 1963.

THE FIGHT FOR CIVIL RIGHTS

The Declaration of Independence (adopted in 1776) said that all men are created equal and have the same rights to life, liberty, and the pursuit of happiness. However in 1960, this still did not apply to the African American population of the U.S.

The 1960s' civil rights movement tried to change this. As both African Americans and caucasians fought for justice, they often met with violence from those opposed to change.

A key leader in the civil rights movement was Martin Luther King Jr. (1929-68). Born in Atlanta, Georgia, Martin L. King Jr. became a powerful public speaker. His most famous speech repeats the words, "I have a dream," and speaks of his dream of a racially tolerant America. Martin L. King Jr. was assassinated in Memphis, Tennessee, in 1968.

Warhol acted as a camera or mirror. He reflected American society – its celebrities, its name brand products, its political events – without comment.

By making art out of a shocking image, he reminds people of how the media themselves treat these images. The pages of a glossy magazine or newspaper are often filled with contrasting pictures of dreadful events and consumer items. The reader may look at a sleek, new car advertisement on one page, and a news article and photograph about a gruesome murder on the next.

In his art, Warhol uses exactly the same multiple and contradictory imagery produced by the global media – magazines, newspapers, TV, and film.

'65 Pontiac Grand Prix.
Now the only question is: who has the year's second-best-looking car?

▲ The U.S. experienced both great affluence and violence in the '60s. While the consumer society flourished, political leaders were assassinated and cities burned in race riots.

TIMELINE ▶

April 1963	August 1963	1963	November 1963	January 1964	1964
Fighting breaks out between civil rights protesters and police in Birmingham, Alabama.	Martin Luther King Jr. addresses over 200,000 people in Washington D.C.	Gerard Malanga becomes Warhol's new assistant.	President Kennedy is assassinated in Dallas, Texas.	Warhol moves to a larger studio on 231 East 47th Street.	Velvet Underground begin to rehearse at the Factory.

Birmingham Race Riot, 1964

screen-print on woven paper, 200 x 240 in (508 x 610 cm), Private Collection

In April of 1963, people protesting peacefully against racial segregation laws were arrested in Birmingham, Alabama, and this led to fighting. Warhol produced a number of different images of the riots which capture the brutal way many police officers treated the unarmed protesters.

"If you want to know all about Warhol, just look at the surface of my paintings and films ... and there I am. There's nothing behind it."

Andy Warhol

The Factory

By 1963 Warhol's townhouse studio had become cluttered and impossible to work in. In June he moved his studio to East 87th Street and employed a young poet, Gerard Malanga, as his assistant. The following year he moved again, to 231 East 47th Street. Here his rented loft became both home and workshop for an enthusiastic group of helpers.

The people working with Warhol included artists, poets, students, and filmmakers. They all exchanged ideas, creating an exciting and fertile atmosphere in which to work. A number of people were responsible for the printing and often carried out every stage of producing works to Warhol's designs. The loft soon became known as the Factory.

▲ Andy Warhol on the Factory fire escape, c.1965.

▲ Warhol's parties were famous.

"Famous people had started to come by the studio, to peek at the ongoing party."

Andy Warhol

TRENDSETTER

In many ways the Factory was like the workshop of a Renaissance artist, with Warhol as the Master. It became the focus for Warhol's fast-moving Pop art scene, and soon was the trendiest place in New York.

The Factory had its own photographers who captured events at the studio on film. A photographer called Billy Name became the Factory foreman. He decorated the inside of the loft with metallic silver paint and aluminium foil, and installed lighting and a sound system.

The Factory was very fashionable among young people. It gained a reputation for weird "happenings," wild parties, and the bad behavior of its guests (although many of Warhol's friends suggested this image was simply an attempt by Warhol to publicize himself).

As a result, the Factory became a meeting place for many different people who wanted to be part of the hip social and creative scene. Celebrities mixed with poets, models with academics, photographers with musicians.

Warhol's friend, the art expert Henry Geldzahler, remembered the Factory as "a sort of glamorous clubhouse with everyone trying to attract Andy's attention. The big question was, whom Andy would notice." This became increasingly important during the mid 1960s, as Warhol began to get involved in filmmaking.

FACTORY FILMS

Between '65 and '74 Paul Morrissey worked at the Factory on Warhol's films. Morrissey arranged screen-tests which involved taking still pictures of new faces among the Factory crowd. Warhol then used them in his films.

He picked out the fashionable model Edie Sedgwick, dazzled by her wealth, beauty, glamour, and style. She became the first in a succession of Factory "superstars."

Eventually the Factory lost its freshness. It became just another part of the New York social scene. In 1968 Warhol moved to a new loft studio at 33 Union Square West. This time he had the interior, which occupied the whole sixth floor, painted entirely in white.

EDIE SEDGWICK

The young model, born in Santa Barbara, California, in 1943, was first attracted to the Warhol crowd in about 1965. She came from a wealthy family and enjoyed the celebrity lifestyle that went with her modeling career. She was close friends with Warhol and others working at the Factory.

Between '65 and '67 Edie Sedgwick starred in many of Warhol's films, including *Poor Little Rich Girl* and *Chelsea Girls*. Although she was happy at the Factory, arguments with Warhol about the small amount of money he paid her to act in his films led them to break up in the late 1960s.

Edie's dependency on drugs then worsened. She moved back to Santa Barbara for treatment, but died suddenly on November 15, 1971. She was just 28 years old.

▶ Edie Sedgwick, late 1960s. Edie had a promising modeling career but really wanted to be in the movies.

Uncertain Times

I n 1964 a *Brillo Box* installation, such as the one shown on the right, was the star of Warhol's second exhibition at the Stable Gallery in Manhattan, New York.

Time magazine reported that Warhol first had the idea for his *Brillo Boxes* in a supermarket. "He was overcome with envy and a sense of beauty. So he had a carpenter make 120 Brillo-sized boxes, and ordered a silk-screen stencil of the Brillo design. He stenciled it on all the boxes ... for his current show, where they are selling for $300 each."

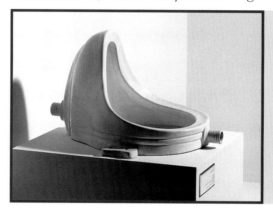

◀ *Fountain* (signed R. Mutt), Marcel Duchamp, 1917. Duchamp created his "ready-mades" by selecting an ordinary item, in this case a urinal. He exhibited the piece without altering it in any way.

WAR IN VIETNAM

In 1963 the U.S., fearing the spread of Communism, sent troops to help South Vietnam which was engaged in civil war with Communist North Vietnam.

Thousands of young Americans were drafted to fight in a distant and unpopular war.

Warhol did not serve, nor was he an anti-war activist. He made very few political statements: "I don't worry about art or life. I mean, the war and the bomb worry me but usually there's not much you can do about them."

The U.S. withdrew from South Vietnam in 1973. In 1975, South Vietnam became part of the Socialist Republic of Vietnam.

MARCEL DUCHAMP

Warhol's inspiration did not just spring from a supermarket shelf. The French artist Marcel Duchamp (1887-1968) had the idea of creating "ready-mades" back in 1913, and shifted people's perceptions of what could be called "art."

Warhol's *Brillo Boxes* explores the same idea. At a time of uncertainty for the U.S., Warhol's art raised unsettling questions about concepts long taken for granted.

WAR, PATRIOTS, AND PROTESTERS

During the mid and late 1960s, controversy over U.S. military involvement in Vietnam tore the country in two. For every American who was proud to do his or her patriotic duty, there were thousands of others, often young students, who protested vigorously against military involvement.

▲ U.S. soldiers in Vietnam watch as helicopters pass overhead.

TIMELINE ▶

January 1964	April 1964	April 1964	August 1964
Warhol exhibits his "Death and Disaster" series at the Sonnabend gallery in Paris.	Warhol creates *Thirteen Most Wanted Men* for the New York State Pavilion at the New York World Fair. The mural was later painted over by Warhol.	The "Brillo Boxes" are exhibited at the Stable Gallery, New York.	Conflict in Vietnam escalates. The U.S. sends troops to fight in South Vietnam.

Brillo Boxes, 1964

silk-screen ink and acrylic on wood,
20 x 20 x 17 in (51 x 51 x 43 cm),
The Andy Warhol Foundation for the
Visual Arts, New York, New York

These oversized boxes, piled up in no obvious order, were revolutionary in their time. They made people question the meaning of the word "art."

"I'm painting this way because I want to be a machine ... anyone else can reproduce the design as well as I could."

Andy Warhol

A Grieving Widow

John F. Kennedy was sworn in as President on January 20, 1961 (see photo below). At the age of 43 he was the youngest elected U.S. president.

His term in office had a difficult start. In April of 1961, he faced international criticism over a failed invasion of Cuba at the Bay of Pigs, and the following year the world drew closer than ever before to nuclear war during the Cuban Missile Crisis. However, in 1963 tensions eased, and the U.S., Great Britain, and the former Soviet Union signed the first treaty banning the testing of nuclear weapons.

Kennedy's assassination was mourned all over the world, and millions tuned in to watch his funeral procession on television.

When John F. Kennedy (known as JFK) was elected President in 1960, he and his wife Jackie seemed to represent a new age in U.S. politics. They were young, glamorous, and attractive.

Three years later, on November 22, 1963, JFK was assassinated by a sniper's bullet in Dallas, Texas.

▲ A photo taken minutes before JFK's assassination. The presidential couple are traveling in an open-topped car past cheering crowds.

During the funeral Jackie was photographed crying beside her husband's coffin. The image of her grief was seen around the world in newspapers, magazines, and on television. Warhol used this photo in 1964 in *Sixteen Jackies* (right). However, he also included photographs of Jackie smiling.

The contrast between the two emotions in the picture is more powerful than a single image would have been. These images show how Jackie's life changed instantly from happiness to sorrow.

Warhol's own attitude, as always, was unusual. He said, "It didn't bother me that he [JFK] was dead. What bothered me was the way the television and radio were programming everybody to be so sad."

▲ President Kennedy takes the oath of office, January 1961.

TIMELINE ▶

Spring 1964	Summer 1964	October 1964	November 1964
Warhol works at the Factory on the "Jackie" series.	Warhol acquires a tape recorder on to which he records diary entries and interviews.	Dr. Martin Luther King Jr. receives the Nobel Peace Prize.	Fighting in Vietnam becomes fiercer. Martial law is declared in Saigon, capital of South Vietnam.

Sixteen Jackies, 1964

Synthetic polymer paint and silk-screen ink on canvas, 80 x 63 $^7/_8$ in (203 x 162 cm), The Brant Foundation, Greenwich, Connecticut

These faces were familiar from endless television screenings. In combination they create a powerful impression of grief.

Warhol and Film

Between 1963 and 1986 Warhol produced 83 films. Most of them are very strange and not what movie-goers usually expect.

For example, some of his early films are completely wordless and very long. They include *Sleep*, a six-hour film made in 1963 by simply pointing the camera at John Giorno as he slept. Other early non-mainstream films that Warhol directed and produced are *Eat* (1963), *Haircut* (1963), and *Kitchen* (1965).

"It's the movies that have really been running things in America ever since they were invented. They show you what to do, how to do it, when to do it, how to feel about it, and how to look how you feel about it."

Andy Warhol

ANTI-HOLLYWOOD

Warhol was aware of how Hollywood dominated the U.S. film industry and deliberately tried to make his films different.

Unlike Hollywood films, Warhol's films rarely have a clear story with a beginning, a middle, and an end.

In the same way, very few of the people who appear in his films were professional actors. Warhol's stars usually came from the Factory, and included Edie Sedgwick (see page 27), the "superstar" Viva, Billy Name (see page 26), and Joe Dallesandro, star of *Lonesome Cowboys* (1967) and *Trash* (1970).

◀ Warhol created this print by placing together two stills from his film *Sleep*, 1965, one above the other.

TIMELINE ▶

1965	October 1965	1966	1967
Warhol produces many films including *Kitchen*, *Poor Little Rich Girl*, and *Sleep*. Race riots in Los Angeles.	Warhol exhibition at the University of Pennsylvania. Also in Toronto and Turin.	Warhol accompanies Velvet Underground to various live performances. First showing of *Chelsea Girls*. Morrissey takes over the direction of Warhol's films.	Warhol and Morrissey travel to the Cannes Film Festival. Warhol begins lecturing at colleges. Produces "Electric Chair" series.

A DIFFERENT KIND OF EXPERIENCE

Films such as *Kitchen* (1963) show ordinary people doing and talking about everyday things. According to Warhol, his films were not intended to entertain but, instead, to allow people in the audience to get to know each other. Warhol thought that if the audience saw something strange on the screen, they were likely to turn to each other to discuss it.

Warhol also said that his films allowed people to do other things like eat, drink, cough, look away, or look back – and find everything still there. This is largely because of the way the camera is used. In many of Warhol's early films the camera concentrates on one object or person, allowing the audience to look at things they might not notice, such as the props, costumes, and lighting. The camera movement, when it does occur, is often shaky or out of focus; and, as with Warhol's silk-screen prints, images are often repeated.

▲ Warhol behind the camera in 1968. Many of the early films were directed by Warhol himself. In later years, Morrissey took over this role.

▲ A publicity photo for the 1970 film, *Trash*. Warhol is seated in the center, and the film's director, Paul Morrissey, on the left.

SHOWING THE FILMS

Warhol also used to show his films in unusual or different ways. Sometimes he showed two films at the same time, either next to or above each other.

AT THE BOX OFFICE

Warhol's first film success was *Chelsea Girls*, released in 1966. This featured visits by artists, musicians, and writers to the famous Chelsea Hotel in New York.

Soon after, Warhol handed over the role of director to his assistant Paul Morrissey. Morrissey worked with Warhol until 1974, and made several commercially successful films including *Trash* (1970).

Productive Years

▲ Russian tanks in Prague, August 1968. It shocked the world that the Russians would invade such a peaceful, cosmopolitan city.

In the mid '60s, Warhol was like a powerhouse. He was involved in a wide range of artistic activities, from art, to film, to music. He generally managed to be commercially successful at everything he tried. He once said that "being good in business is the most fascinating kind of art."

Whatever the art form, Warhol wanted to keep artistic intervention to a minimum. He wanted to reflect the world without putting a message on what he showed. For him, the interest of filmmaking lay in this lack of intervention: all the work was done by the camera, the subject it was pointing at, and the person watching the film.

RUSSIAN INVASION

During the summer of 1968, while he was recovering from his gunshot wounds, Warhol watched lots of television. On August 22nd, he saw footage showing the Russians invading Czechoslovakia, the country where his parents were born.

The invasion by heavily-armed Soviet troops was in response to attempts by Alexander Dubcek, leader of the Czechoslovak Communist Party, to introduce liberal social reforms including more freedom for the media, a period known as "the Prague spring" (Prague was the capital of Czechoslovakia).

Dubcek's reforms were stopped by the Russians. It would take another 20 years, until 1989, before Czechoslavakia finally freed itself from Soviet control.

▲ Valerie Solanis being interviewed by journalists following her arrest for the attempted murder of Andy Warhol, 1968.

ATTACK AT THE FACTORY

On June 3, 1968, Warhol was the victim of an assassination attempt. Valerie Solanis, the sole member of SCUM (Society for the Cutting Up of Men), tried to kill him. Luckily she failed, but two bullets entered Warhol's lungs, stomach, liver, and throat. He was in the hospital for two months.

TIMELINE ▶

February 1968	April 1968	June 1968	August 1968
Warhol moves to a new studio at 33 Union Square West, New York.	Dr. Martin Luther King Jr. is shot dead in Memphis, Tennessee.	Warhol is shot at his studio by Valerie Solanis. He survives but spends the next two months in the hospital.	The Russians invade Czechoslovakia following its attempts to reform hard-line Communist policies.

Stills From *Empire*, 1964

Warhol's film *Empire*, made in 1964, is eight hours long. It is completely silent, and focuses on a single view of the Empire State Building in New York (at the time this was the tallest building in the world).

The film shows one view of the building for a whole day, from sunrise to sunset. Many critics thought the film was too long.

"My films using stationary objects were made to help the audience get more acquainted with themselves."

Andy Warhol

Back to the Beginning

INTERVIEW MAGAZINE

Andy Warhol's *Interview* was the first magazine to focus on revealing interviews of celebrities, including film star Elizabeth Taylor, boxer Muhammad Ali, and politician Henry Kissinger.

At first Warhol was not involved much. However, as the magazine became more successful, he began conducting interviews himself. He was also able to attend parties with the celebrities, taking their pictures with his Polaroid camera.

Interview used very modern page designs and elegant, or sometimes experimental photos. By the 1980s it had become an art form in its own right.

▲ Warhol with Mick Jagger, lead singer of the British rock group the Rolling Stones.

▲ Warhol (front left) with some of the staff of *Interview*, in a photo taken to advertise the magazine, c.1978.

After the attempt on his life, Warhol's attitude and the way he dealt with the people around him changed completely. Access to the Factory at 33 Union Square West, was restricted to a very small circle of friends.

Warhol returned to his previous success as an artist, creating portraits of well-known people such as the leader of Communist China, Mao-Tse Tung (in 1972), and the famous American writer Truman Capote (in 1979). He spent less and less time with the "unknown" faces at the Factory.

In 1969 Warhol was asked by John Wilcock, editor of the underground newspaper *Other Scenes*, to work with him to produce a new magazine. The first issue of *Interview* appeared in the autumn of 1969.

RENEWING OLD THEMES

Throughout the 1970s Warhol continued to work, producing silk-screen images and experimenting with new techniques. In the early 1980s, returning to a much earlier theme (see pages 10-11), he produced a series of silk-screen shoe pictures such as the one opposite.

TIMELINE ▶

1969	1969-72	1972-78	1978-79
First landing on the moon. Vietnam war intensifies. Warhol exhibition in Berlin. First issue of *Interview*.	Warhol produces relatively few new works, other than portraits of artist friends and gallery owners, and a few commissions.	Warhol mainly produces portraits, and continues to re-work old pictures. A number of exhibitions around the world.	Warhol produces "Oxidation" and "Shadows" series. Meets Joseph Beuys. Shah of Iran overthrown. Russians invade Afghanistan.

Diamond Dust Shoes, 1980

screen-print with diamond dust, 40 x 59 ²/₅ in (102 x 151 cm), Private Collection

Warhol produced a number of diamond dust pictures, including a series of "Shadows" in 1979 and portraits of the German artist Joseph Beuys (see page 42) in 1980. He created these magical paintings by sprinkling powdered crystal, or "diamond dust," on to the wet silk-screened canvas.

It's possible to see the sparkling dust in the black areas of the picture, but the canvas has to be seen in a gallery to appreciate this dazzling effect.

"I still care about people but it would be so much easier not to care ... it's too hard to care."

Andy Warhol

Self-Portrait

▲ Warhol photographed before a gueststar appearance on the television show *Love Boat*, c.1984.

As well as painting, photography, and filmmaking, Warhol also wrote or contributed to several books including his famous *POPism. The Warhol '60s*. This was a transcript of his diary entries, made using a tape recorder, from 1964 onward. In 1985 he published *America*, one of several collections of his photographs, featuring pictures of New York City and his trips across the United States.

THE FINAL PERFORMANCE

Most of Warhol's later works focus on the concept of "Warhol" himself, and explore ideas related to death. His series of "Self-Portraits," including the one on the right, were exhibited in 1986 at the Anthony d'Offay Gallery in London. In 1987 he produced a series of "Last Supper" pictures which were shown at the Palazzo delle Stelline in Milan.

Warhol once said that dying was the most embarrassing thing one could do. On February 22, 1987, Andy Warhol embarrassed all his friends by dying unexpectedly at New York Hospital-Cornell Medical Center following surgery for a routine gallbladder operation. He was only 58 years old.

15 MINUTES OF FAME

On several occasions during the 1970s Warhol said, "The great unfulfilled ambition of my life is to have my own regular TV show." He achieved this ambition in 1980, when the talk show *Andy Warhol's TV* was aired on cable stations. The show ran until 1982.

In 1986, he appeared on TV again when *Andy Warhol's Fifteen Minutes* was aired on MTV. Taking its title from Warhol's most famous saying (see opposite), the show attracted an enthusiastic teenage audience, and made Warhol popular with a whole new generation.

Warhol the artist had finally become Warhol the celebrity.

▲ Andy Warhol was buried in Pittsburgh. The funeral was a small, private ceremony with only family members and close friends invited.

TIMELINE ▶

1980	1981-86	1986	1987
Warhol does portrait of Beuys. *Andy Warhol's TV* aired on TV. *POPism. The Warhol '60s* published.	Warhol does advertising work. Continues with portraits and some new works including "Dollar Signs," "Crosses," and "Guns."	*Andy Warhol's 15 Minutes* aired on MTV. Produces "Camouflage," "Cars," "Lenin," "Last Supper," and "Self-Portrait" series.	On February 22nd, Andy Warhol dies in New York as a result of surgery.

Self-Portrait, 1986

synthetic polymer paint and silk-screen on canvas, 40 x 40 in (101.6 x 101.6 cm), The Andy Warhol Museum, Pittsburgh, Pennsylvania

Warhol made self-portraits throughout his career. The picture above includes a camouflage element he created for a separate series of pictures in 1986. Warhol has altered the camouflage pattern to include the patriotic colors red, white, and blue. The irregular stripes partially hide his face while at the same time merging with it. Warhol seems to be saying that he is a part of American culture itself.

"In the future everyone will be famous for 15 minutes."

Andy Warhol

Warhol's Legacy

Andy Warhol was one of the most important artists of the 20th century. His involvement in art was not just about painting, but included all other aspects of the art world such as advertising, film, television, music, journalism, literature, consumer products, and money.

MEDIA MAN

Warhol was multi-talented and worked successfully across different types of media. He made paintings and films, organized a workshop of artists, wrote books, edited a magazine, and put together a rock band.

A product of the 20th century, Warhol responded to the widespread availability of media images seen in magazines, comics, newspaper, TV, and film. Later, they reflected his own fame back to him.

Warhol was famous not only for his art, but also for being a celebrity. In many ways he was as famous as the celebrities he admired so much.

POP ARTIST

Warhol embodied Pop art – its reflection of a throwaway consumer society, and its attitude to life and culture.

In simple direct images he summarized the themes of mid-20th century America.

His mass-produced images reflected the mass-production of consumer goods. They seem to suggest that art was simply another consumer product, while at the same time making us wonder if it was true or not.

▲ A Warhol Family Museum of Modern Art was established in 1991 in Medzilaborce, just outside Mikova, Slovakia, the birthplace of Warhol's parents.

"Andy Warhol's name is a household word. The ghostly complexion, the silver-white hair, the dark glasses, and the leather jacket combine to make a memorable image ... Warhol's greatest artwork is 'Andy Warhol'."

Art critic John Perrault

▲ Damien Hirst's *Pharmacy* opened in 1998, but was criticized because it looked too much like a real pharmacy. He then changed the name to *Army Chap* (an anagram of pharmacy).

NO COMMENT

Warhol challenged ideas about what art is and how people are supposed to respond to it.

Unlike many artists who speak at length on exactly what they are trying to do, expressing their aims and artistic intentions, and often their tortured souls, Andy Warhol was reluctant to say anything at all about his art. He left it entirely up to the viewer to respond to it in whatever way they wanted.

DAMIEN HIRST

Like Warhol, the British artist Damien Hirst (b.1965) is a celebrity painter. He became famous in London in the 1990s as one of the leading figures in what became known as Britart.

Like Warhol, many of Hirst's images are about death – some of his most memorable artworks show dead animals preserved in formaldehyde. In their simplicity his paintings, which show colored circles on a white background, are also like Warhol's.

Hirst also extends his art beyond the canvas. He makes installations, creates artworks which look like specimens from a natural history museum, directs videos for pop groups, and has been involved in the restaurant trade. His restaurant, *Pharmacy*, in London's trendy Notting Hill was named after one of his installation pieces which resembled a drug store. Confusingly, the *Pharmacy* restaurant he designed looked exactly like the inside of a pharmacy.

ANDY WARHOL MUSEUM

The Andy Warhol Museum was established in Warhol's birthplace, in Pittsburgh, Pennsylvania, in 1994. The museum features a number of permanent exhibits and holds over 4,000 examples of Warhol's work. These include paintings, drawings, prints, photographs, sculptures, films, and videotapes.

▲ The Andy Warhol Museum is one of the four Carnegie Museums of Pittsburgh. It is a joint project of the Carnegie Institute, Dia Center for the Arts, and The Andy Warhol Foundation.

Pop Art, Performance Art

The famous German Performance artist Joseph Beuys first met Warhol in 1979. Beuys admired Warhol, and in 1980 he commissioned him to do his portrait. Warhol used diamond dust for it (see page 37). The portraits toured Europe, opening in Naples in April of 1980, followed by Munich and then Geneva. As a result, both of the artists received a lot of publicity.

▶ Andy Warhol, center, in New York with Joseph Beuys (left). On the right is the American artist Robert Rauschenberg (b. 1925).

He was a real revolutionary artist without probably understanding it in the correct way ... he had this intuitive feeling and was saying more about society in a political sense than many other artists who made direct political statements.

▲ Joseph Beuys about Andy Warhol, 1979.

(see page 37)

JOSEPH BEUYS

Beuys was born in Germany in 1921 and went on to become one of the leading artists in the Performance art movement – art which combined theater, music, and visual arts.

One of his most famous performances was called *How to Explain Pictures to a Dead Hare*, 1965. For it, Beuys walked around a gallery with his face painted in gold and cradled a dead hare in his arms.

In much the same way as Warhol, Beuys contributed to his own fame by making his life appear mysterious and strange. He led the way in moving public attention from an artist's work to focus on his or her personality and actions.

By the time of his death in 1986, Joseph Beuys was an international celebrity.

TIMELINE ▶

1928	1949	1957	1962	1962	1963
August 6, 1928 Andrew Warhola is born in Forest City, Pennsylvania. **1945** World War II ends. **1945-49** Studies at the Carnegie Institute of Technology, Pittsburgh. Has summer job in a department store. Visits New York.	**1949** Works in New York as a commercial artist. Shortens his name to Andy Warhol. **1952** First exhibition in New York. Success as a commercial artist. **1956** Wins the 36th Annual Art Directors' Club Award for a shoe advertisement.	**1957** Has plastic surgery on his nose. **1960** Begins to paint using blown-up cartoon strips. **1961** Creates pictures of Campbell's soup cans. **1962** Lichtenstein exhibits his cartoon artwork.	**1962** Warhol starts using photo silk-screen printing. **Summer 1962** Begins work on the "Death and Disaster" series. **August 1962** Exhibits 32 pictures of Campbell's soup cans in Los Angeles. Buys them himself.	**1962** Following the death of Marilyn Monroe in August, begins the "Marilyn" series. **October 1962** Exhibits at the Pop art exhibition "The New Realists" in New York. **November 1962** First solo exhibition in New York.	**1963** Speech by Martin Luther King Jr. Gerard Malanga becomes assistant. **November 1963** President Kennedy is assassinated in Dallas. **1964** Warhol moves to the Factory. Begins to work with Velvet Underground. Exhibits the "Brillo Boxes."

▲ Andy Warhol about Joseph Beuys, 1980.

CREATING A MYTH

Beuys, like Warhol, was not simply an artist, but also a showman, co-founder of the Green party in Germany, and someone who turned his own life into a myth. One of Beuys's claims was that during the war (in which he served as a German pilot) he was shot down over the Russian tundra. According to him, nomads found him and nursed him back to health, protecting him with fat and wrapping him in felt. Later, he used these materials in his art.

WORKING TOGETHER

Warhol was not interested in Beuys's work to begin with, but he began to take notice when Beuys became more famous. Beuys helped Warhol to be taken seriously in Germany and across Europe. Each improved the other's reputation.

In March of 1982, Warhol exhibited in Berlin with Beuys, Rauschenberg, and Cy Twombley (b.1929). So many people wanted to see the exhibition that there were fears about public safety, and the police had to close the show on opening day.

THE PRICE IS RIGHT?

At the end of 1983, the statistician Dr. Bongard published his annual list of the top 100 artists based on the value of their works, according to the prices paid at auctions. Beuys topped the list, Warhol came second, and Rauschenberg third.

▲ Andy Warhol, in conversation with the Hollywood actress Jodie Foster.

1964	1966	1968	1969-72	1978	1982-86
1964 Conflict in Vietnam escalates. Warhol works on the "Jackie" series. Starts recording diary entries and interviews on a tape recorder. The Factory is scene of trendy "happenings." Films *Empire*. **1965** Produces many films. Race riots in Los Angeles.	**1965** First showing of *Chelsea Girls*. Morrissey takes over as film director. **1967** Travels to the Cannes Film Festival. Begins lecturing at colleges. Produces "Electric Chair" series. **April 1968** Martin Luther King Jr. is shot dead in Memphis.	**June 1968** Warhol is shot and spends two months in hospital. **August 1968** Russians invade Czechoslovakia. **1969** First landing on the moon. Vietnam war intensifies. Warhol exhibition in Berlin. First issue of *Interview*.	**1969-72** Few new works, other than portraits of artist friends and gallery owners, and some commissions. **1972-78** Mainly produces portraits but also continues to re-work old pictures. A number of Warhol exhibitions are held around the world.	**1978** Produces "Oxidation" and "Shadows" series. **1979** Meets Joseph Beuys. **1980** Portrait of Beuys. *Andy Warhol's TV* is screened on TV. *POPism. The Warhol '60s* is published. **1981** Several new works including "Dollar Signs."	**1982-86** Returns to advertising work, more portraits. Many exhibitions are held. **1986** *Andy Warhol's 15 Minutes* screened on MTV. Produces "Camouflage," "Cars," and "Self-Portrait." **February 22, 1987** Andy Warhol dies in a New York hospital as result of surgery.

Glossary

Abstract Expressionism: the name given to the work of several artists based in New York in the 1940s and '50s. Their work focused on expressing their emotions and what they were actually feeling as they painted.

aesthetics: the principles or study of artistic taste.

brand: a group of goods from one manufacturer that are recognized by their name, design, or logo.

Britart: a British art movement of the 1990s which echoed many of the themes of Pop art. Its most famous exhibition was called "Sensation" and included artworks that were designed to shock people.

celebrity: someone who is famous.

civil rights: the rights guaranteed by the state to its citizens. Between c. 1954-68, the civil rights movement in the U.S. fought to secure equal civil rights for African Americans.

commercial art: art designed to help sell something, for example, the illustrations used in an advertisement.

Communism: a political system, based on the teachings of Karl Marx (1818-83), that believes in a strong central state and the abolition of private property. In the 20th century, Communism was established in both the former Soviet Union and China, and spread from there into a number of other countries.

consumer society: a society whose main goal is to provide goods and services to the public (the consumer).

Great Depression: the global economic slump of the 1930s.

"happening": a performance in which elements from everyday life are put together in a strange, non-realistic way. Usually the audience is asked to participate.

hip: well informed about the latest fashion or taste.

icon: an image or figure that symbolizes or represents something.

idol: someone or something you worship or admire.

installation: in art, a series of objects or sculptures arranged in a particular way.

interior designer: someone who designs the inside of houses, offices or shops, choosing color schemes, carpets, curtains, etc.

logo: a symbol or trademark used to identify a manufacturer or particular type of goods.

mainstream: in art, what is considered normal.

mass production: a standardized process to manufacture items in large quantities.

media: channels through which information is distributed such as newspapers, magazines, radio, TV, or the internet.

Performance art: a postwar art movement that combined theater, music, and visual art. One of its leading artists was Joseph Beuys (1921-86).

Pop art: an art movement of the 1960s that tried to produce art that everyone would like, and rejected ideas of good and bad taste. Pop art often depicted subjects from popular culture.

popular culture: culture that is enjoyed by the general public, such as pop music, films, and TV.

Renaissance: the period between c. 1400 and 1600 which saw a great revival in all the arts. (From the French word *renaissance* meaning "rebirth.")

screentest: test to decide whether someone will look good on the movie or TV screen.

segregation: separation of one group from another, often on the basis of race or religion.

silk-screen printing: a form of printing in which color ink is forced through a silk mesh onto the surface beneath.

Soviet Union: a federation of Communist republics under the leadership and control of Russia. The Soviet Union was disbanded in 1991.

studio: an artist's workshop.

underground: in art, a social and artistic movement of the 1960s that wanted to change society and make it more free.

Museums and Galleries

Works by Warhol are exhibited in museums and galleries all around the world, although many are held in private collections. Most of the museums and galleries listed here have a wide range of other artists' works on display.

Even if you can't visit any of these galleries yourself, you may be able to visit their web sites. Gallery web sites often show pictures of the artworks they have on display. Some of the web sites even offer virtual tours which allow you to wander around and look at different paintings while sitting comfortably in front of your computer! Most of the international web sites detailed below include an option that allows you to view them in English.

UNITED STATES

The Andy Warhol Museum
117 Sandusky Street
Pittsburgh, PA 15212-5890
www.warhol.org

The Baltimore Museum of Art
10 Art Museum Drive
Baltimore, MD 21218-3898
www.artbma.org

Birmingham Museum of Art
2000 Eighth Avenue North
Birmingham, AL 35203-2278
www.artsbma.org

Carnegie Museum of Art
4400 Forbes Avenue
Pittsburgh, PA 15213-4080
www.cmoa.org

Solomon R. Guggenheim Museum
1071 5th Avenue (at 89th Street)
New York, NY
www.guggenheimcollection.org

EUROPE

Centre National d'Art et de Culture Georges Pompidou
75191 Paris
cedex 04
France
www.centrepompidou.fr

Hungarian National Gallery
Buda Castle, The Royal Palace
Building BCD
2 Szent György Square
Budapest
Hungary

Staatagalerie Stuttgart
Konrad-Adenauer-Str. 30-32
D-70173 Stuttgart
Germany
www.staatsgalerie.de

Tate Modern
Bankside
London
SE1 9TG
England
www.tate.org.uk

Warhol Family Museum of Modern Art
www.slovakia.org/culture-warhol.htm

Index